A

Solid As The ROCK

Contemporary Songs For Youth Choir

Two and Three Part Arrangements by **Dennis Allen**

Dramatic Sketches by **Nan Allen**

LILLENAS PUBLISHING COMPANY
Kansas City, MO 64141

CONTENTS

Beyond Belief

B. H.

BOB HARTMAN
Arr. by Dennis Allen

Leap of faith___ with - out a net___
makes us want___ to hedge our bet.___ Wa - ters nev - er part___ un - til___ our

feet get wet._____ Oh!_____ There's a deep - er place to go,____

where the road__ seems hard to hoe.____ He who has__ be - gun_____ this work__ won't

let it go.____ And it takes so__ long__

once were weak,____ but now we're strong.____

There's a high - er place____ to go, be-yond____ be-lief, be-yond____ be-lief;

Where we reach the next____ pla - teau, be-yond____ be-lief, be-yond____ be-lief.

The Climbers by Nan Allen

Characters: CLIMBERS (5)

Props: backpacks and hiking equipment (canteens, maps, hiking boots, etc.)

(Enter "CLIMBERS 1-4", slowly in single file. They are sadly singing "We Are Climbing Jacob's Ladder", crossing to center stage)

#1: Okay everybody, let's stop and rest for awhile. (CLIMBERS *take off backpacks. They moan and groan as they start to sit and recline)*

#2 *(to #1)*: How far are we from the top?

#1 *(looking offstage)*: Oh, I don't know. I can't even see the top from here.

#3 *(whining)*: Oh man! Seems like we've been climbing forever! My feet hurt.

#4: Yeah. Mine, too. And I'm thirsty.

#2: I thought it would be easier than this.

#1: If you'll remember, we were told that the Christian life might sometimes become a long, hard trip.

#3: But we were also told that it would be worth the effort.

#4: Yeah, where's the reward? All I've gotten so far are fallen arches and a blister on my heel.

#2 *(poking out lower lip)*: I want my mommy.

(#3 and #4 consoles #2; CLIMBERS sit and moan about aches and pains; Enter CLIMBER #5, crosses to center, speaks to CLIMBER #1)

#5: Hey, you guys. Do you mind if I rest here for awhile?

#1: Oh, no. Not at all. Help yourself.

(#5 unloads backpack and begins to "set up camp". He/she is very cheerful, singing "Climb, Climb Up Sunshine Mountain"; other CLIMBERS look at #5 with amazement)

#2 *(to #5)*: Uh, excuse us. We were wondering something.

#5: Oh?

#2: Yeah, we were wondering. Have you been on this journey very long?

#5: Not too long. Probably about the same as you. Why?

#1: Oh, just wondering how you can be so cheerful. We're here at the same spot and we're exhausted and. . .uh, *(looking at the others)* some are starting to complain. (CLIMBERS 2, 3, *and* 4 *point to each other)*

#5: Well, I understand. It's a hard climb. . .and I hear it gets even harder the closer you get to the top.

#3: What?

#4: You mean, it gets worse? I'm out of here!

#5: No, you can't stop now! It's hard, yes, but you get stronger and stronger. The higher you go the more you're able to see things that you could never dream of down at the beginning of the journey.

#2: Like what?

#5: Like blessings and victories. . .

#3 *(sarcastically)*: Oh, sounds like church talk.

#5: Huh, guess it does, maybe at first. But when you look back on where you've come, it starts to make more sense.

#1: Looking back? Why would we want to look back?

#2: Yeah, I thought the Bible said that we should forget what's behind and press forward.

#5: It does. But I always thought that passage of scripture meant we shouldn't be attached to the past. . . don't let the failures get us down, or the victories make us too cocky, you know? Hey, just turn around and look back, only for a second. . .

(CLIMBERS all turn and look in direction of their entrance)

#1: Wow! We've come farther than we think.

#2: And look at all the great things that God's done for us, things we've experienced. . .people we've influenced along the way.

#5: Blessings. . .

#3: Well, I've make a lot of mistakes. . .

#4: Me, too. But, I guess we've learned a lot. . .

#5: Victories. . .

#1 *(to #5)*: Say, it sounds like you're pretty wise. . .

#2 *(to #5)*: Yeah, have you already traveled this road before?

#5: No, no. *(takes out the Bible)* I've just read about a few people who have. . . *(music begins)*

Higher Ground

JOHNSON OATMAN, Jr.

DENNIS ALLEN
Arr. by Dennis Allen

18

Nothing Can Keep Us from His Love

Based on ROMANS 8:31-39

DENNIS and NAN ALLEN
Arr. by Dennis Allen

Extra! Extra! by Nan Allen

Characters:
- NEWSBOY or NEWSGIRL
- #1, average passerby
- #2, executive type
- #3, plain clothes cop

Props:
- newspapers
- briefcase
- badge/ID.
- bus stop sign (optional)

(Scene opens with NEWSBOY/NEWSGIRL *standing at center stage, holding up newspaper)*

NEWSBOY/GIRL: Extra! Extra! Read all about it! Important discovery. Something found that never fades, never rusts, never dies. Extra! Extra! Read about the only thing found to be eternal!

#1: Yeah, right! Another sales pitch? What is it this time? A household appliance? A digital watch? Handy dandy toe nail clippers, just right for your home or office?

NEWSBOY: No, it's. . .

#1: You'll probably tell me to dial 1-800-BIG-DEAL, not available in stores. Well, no thanks. Nothing's that good. . . *(exits)*

NEWSBOY: But. . .it's God's love. Don't you get it? It's. . .oh, well. Extra! Extra! Read all about it! Important discovery. Something found that never fades, never rusts, never dies.

(Enter #2, carrying briefcase)

#2: Is that for real? I mean, is there something that durable that it will last forever?

NEWSBOY: Yes! Let me tell you about it. . .it's. . .

#2: Okay, how much?

NEWSBOY: Pardon me?

#2 *(reaching into pocket)*: How much? Something that good's gotta cost an arm and a leg.

NEWSBOY: No, it's free. . .

#2: Uh huh. Oh, I get it. It's a free sample, a teaser, huh? Get the buying public to a point where they can't live without it, then go into mass production. . .international trade? Pretty clever marketing scheme. Hey, who's your broker?

NEWSBOY: I don't have a broker. I'm not selling anything. Honest, it's free. I'm just getting the word out.

#2: You expect me to believe that there is something that lasts forever? And it's free!? Boy, I've seen some weirdos in my time, but this one tops them all. *(exits)*

NEWSBOY: Extra! Extra! Read all about it. . .

#3: Hey, buddy! *(takes out ID)* Sergeant Sludge. . .Bunko Squad. *(starts to lead* NEWSBOY *away)* Come along quietly, please. We'd like to ask you a few questions down at the station.

NEWSBOY: But what for, officer? I have a permit and a license and even a note from my mother!

#3: Not good enough. You're under arrest. "You have the right to remain silent. Anything you say can and will be used against you in a court of law. . ."

NEWSBOY: Wait a minute, officer. At least tell me what I've done.

#3: Hey, false advertising is a crime in this state!

NEWSBOY: False advertising?

#3: Everybody knows that there's nothing with that kind of guarantee. . .never fade, rust. . .or die?

NEWSBOY: But officer, it's true. I'm talking about God's love. The only thing ever found that never fails.

#3: Wise guy, huh? *(starting to exit with* NEWSBOY*)*

NEWSBOY: Officer, I've got proof. . . hard evidence.

#3: Oh yeah?

NEWSBOY: My life! My life is the proof. . . *(as they exit)*

#3: Tell it to the jury!

NEWSBOY *(music begins)*: Okay then, your life. . . *(fading)* let's talk about you. . .

God's Love Never Changes

D.T. and M.T.

DICK and MELODY TUNNEY
Arr. by Dennis Allen

27

The Love We Know

B. S. and W. K.

BILLY SIMON and WAYNE KIRKPATRICK
Arr. by Dennis Allen

Give the fi - re a stead - y glow and hang on to the love we know.

CD: 23

N.C.

CD: 24 *mf*

Got to hang on to the love we know.

hang on — to the love we know, Can't af - ford — to let — it — go.

Give the fi - re a stead-y glow and hang on to — the love — we — know.

Hang on to — the love — we know!

Advice by Nan Allen

Characters:
SAM
BRIAN

CARRIE
AMY
(or use real names)

Props:
large cardboard box
book

(Enter SAM *carrying large box. He holds it out in front so that it keeps him from seeing what is in front of him, crossing left to right. Enter* BRIAN *reading book, crossing right to left)*

BRIAN *(almost bumping into* Sam*)*: Hey, man. Watch where you're going. You nearly knocked me down.
SAM: Sorry. *(peeking out from behind box)* Oh, hi, Brian.
BRIAN: Well, Sam. Didn't know that was you. How have you been?
SAM *(trying to look happy)*: Oh, fine. *(suddenly sad)* Well, actually I'm kinda down right now. Ya see,
    I've got this burden I'm carrying. . .
BRIAN: Oh yeah. I noticed that. It looks heavy.
SAM: It is. . .and sometimes it kind of blinds me to things that are going on around me.
BRIAN: I noticed that, too. You nearly ran me down. Say, would you like some help from an old friend?
SAM: Yeah, please. I'd love some. *(tries to give box to* BRIAN*)*
BRIAN: Oh, no. Not that kind of help. I have a bad back. But I thought you might like some advice.
    (philosophically, showing SAM *the book he's reading.)* You see, according to Dr. C. Edwin
    Newburg it would seem to me that you have a deep inner need syndrome that has brought you all
    these problems. Dr. C. Edwin Newburg would suggest that you are, in fact, a product of your
    own inhibitions.
SAM *(staring blankly)*: Uh huh, thanks.
BRIAN: Hey, what are friends for? *(pats* SAM *on back and then exits)*
SAM: That's a good question.
(Enter CARRIE *from behind* SAM *overtaking him)*
CARRIE: Well, look who's here. Haven't seen you in a hundred years. What have you been up to?
SAM: I've had some problems. . .a syndrome thing. . .and well, I'm kind of burdened right now.
CARRIE: I see you could use some help. After all, what are friends for? Can I give you some advice?
SAM: Is it from Dr. C. Edwin Newburg?
CARRIE: What?
SAM: Never mind.
CARRIE: See, you're carrying that burden all wrong. If you carried it say. . .on your head for instance,
    you could smile all the time and probably no one would notice that you've got a problem. Or
    maybe carry it out to one side or strap it to your back. That's it, strap it to your back. It would
    leave your hands free. At least you could be productive while you're burdened. Well, it's good to
    see you again. Take care! *(exits)*
*(*SAM *awkwardly tries a few of the positions that* CARRIE *recommended. Enter* AMY*)*
AMY: Hello.
SAM *(sadly)*: Oh, hi. . .Amy
AMY *(genuinely concerned)*: How are you?
SAM: You want the honest truth?
AMY: Looks like you're carrying around some problems there.
SAM: Yeah, and they're getting heavier and heavier.
AMY: Well, can I help you?
SAM: Uh no, I've had all the advice and evaluations I need for awhile.
AMY: I wasn't gonna give you advice. I was going to ask if I could help you carry your burden.
SAM *(brightens for a moment, then looks sad)*: Actually, this is something I guess I need to carry alone.
AMY: But. . .I'd like to help. Tell me how.
SAM: Well, for starters you could keep your advice to yourself.
AMY: Okay. I can do that.
SAM: I know, most of these problems are my fault; apparently I've even been carrying them wrong, too.
AMY: Ah, no big deal.
SAM: So you really want to help?
AMY: Sure.
SAM *(as they exit)*: Maybe you could just walk along beside me for a while. . .and we could talk. . .and
    maybe you could even pray for me. . .and be there to listen. . .and help me up when I fall. . .
AMY: Hey, what are friends for? *(music begins)*

I'm Prayin' for You

D. T. and M. T.

DICK and MELODY TUNNEY
Arr. by Dennis Allen

With feeling, out of tempo

* Song may begin at measure 5 if desired.

40

Lyrics (vocal line):
we can bear. So be-cause___ I be-lieve___ God is
lis-t'nin', I'm pray-in'___ for you.

CD: 29

3. With

CD: 31

44

Why?

M.H., D.K., and D.C.

MARK HARRIS, DON KOCH, and DAVE CLARK
Arr. by Dennis Allen

Solo (opt. unison choir) *mf*

They say that in-to ev - 'ry life some rain must fall,_____ for the pain is no re-spect - er of the

49

Lord has nev - er been__ a - fraid of hon - est prayers,_____ and He

won't al - low the bur - den to be more than you__ can bear._____ When He

knows that your trust is in Him, He does - n't mind___ the

The Care Package
By Nan Allen

Characters:
>LESLIE
>ROBERT, the skeptic
>CATHERINE
>JON

Props:
>large box or package
>teddy bear
>large sponge
>door knob
>jar of peanut butter
>Bible
>envelope

(Scene opens with box or package at center stage. Characters enter talking to each other)

LESLIE *(noticing package at center)*: Hey, look, you guys! A package. It must have come while we were out.

ROBERT: Oh cool. Who's it for?

CATHERINE *(reading from package)*: Says here. . ."Care Package." It's addressed to. . ."Everybody" it says.

ROBERT: Everybody? What's that suppose to mean?

JON: You know. . .everybody. . .us!

ROBERT: Yeah? But who's it from?

CATHERINE: Doesn't say that. Just says "Care Package."

LESLIE: Let's open it.

ROBERT: No! We might get in trouble.

CATHERINE: Trouble?

ROBERT: Yeah, it could have an alarm on it. . .or maybe it's booby trapped!

JON (grabbing the package): Let's see.

(Open package, all look inside and gasp)

JON: It's a teddy bear!

ROBERT *(suspiciously)*: Is it ticking?

CATHERINE: No, it's not ticking. Hey, there's some other stuff in the bottom.

LESLIE: Wow! It's a. . .a. . .doorknob?

JON: And a sponge. . .

CATHERINE: . . .and a jar of peanut butter.

ROBERT: That Jason. I knew he'd get me sooner or later.

JON: Jason? You mean our youth director Jason? *(OR use the name of your youth director/leader)*

ROBERT: Yeah, on youth retreat I put some shaving cream in his gym socks.

LESLIE *(rolling her eyes)*: Oh, brother! How juvenile!

ROBERT: He laughed about it. Said it was okay. But I know he's playing a trick on me, just to get even. This whole thing will probably explode any minute.

LESLIE: This doesn't look like a joke, Robert. And it doesn't say anything about Jason.

CATHERINE: It looks more like a riddle. . .

JON: or a coded message. . .like Mercury Man on TV. He's always figuring out coded messages.

ROBERT: There's something else in there. . .*(pinching his nostrils)*. . .probably a stink bomb!

CD: 40

2nd time to Coda

catch-es ev - 'ry tear.   Je - sus   cares.

Prom - is - es___ get bro - ken,   trust can be___ be - trayed.

An - gry words___ are spo - ken   and leave a heart___ in pain.   But

CD: 43

cries of pain and fear.   He catch - es ev - 'ry tear.   Je - sus

Je - sus cares, _____ that's break - ing.   Je - sus cares, _____
cares   for ev - 'ry heart that's break - ing.   Je - sus cares _____ for

_____ that's break - ing.
ev - 'ry heart that's break - ing.   Je - sus   cares.

Stand Up and Bless the Lord

64

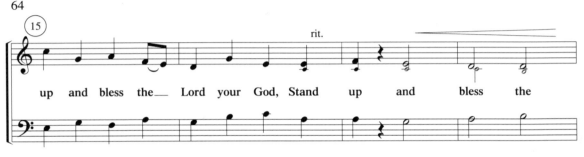

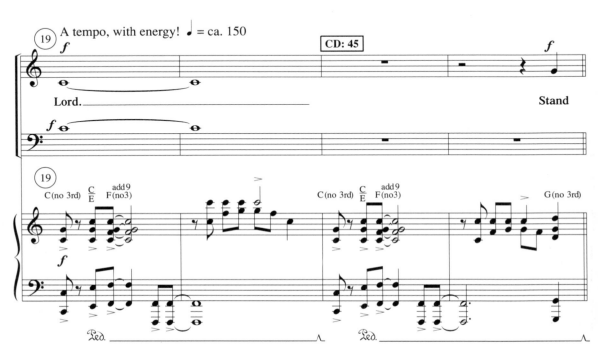

68

Prize Fight
by Nan Allen

Characters:
>THE ACCUSER
>THE ATONER
>THE CHRISTIAN

Props:
>chair
>high stool
>Bible

Setting: THE CHRISTIAN is seated at center stage in a regular chair. He or she is reading a Bible. THE ACCUSER sits on the stage at the Christian's right. THE ATONER sits on a high stool to the Christian's left. THE ACCUSER wears black clothing (or jeans and a black shirt). THE ATONER wears white.

(Scene opens as THE ATONER *and* THE ACCUSER *take their places, freezing into place. Enter* THE CHRISTIAN, *sits in center stage chair, begins to read Bible.)*

THE ACCUSER *(to* CHRISTIAN, *sarcastically)*: Soooo. . .reading the Good Book, are we? Nothing good on TV, I guess? *(*CHRISTIAN *does not respond)* What a way to spend an afternoon! *(*CHRISTIAN *continues to read silently)*

THE ATONER *(to* CHRISTIAN*)*: I'm really glad you came. I've got a few things I want to tell you . . .
>*(*CHRISTIAN *continues to read silently)*

THE ACCUSER *(to* CHRISTIAN*)*: What is it, today? *(craning neck to see Bible)* Oh, the Beatitudes I see. *(sarcastically)* Good choice. . .for wimps! *(mockingly)* "Blessed are the poor in spirit. . .blessed are the meek. . ." Wake up, man. Smell the coffee. Nice guys finish last!

THE ATONER *(to* CHRISTIAN*)*: Ah, my Sermon on the Mount! One of my favorites. I was trying to tell people. . .then and now. . .that happiness is something that only I can give them. . .

THE CHRISTIAN *(aloud)*: "Blessed are those who hunger and thirst for righteousness. . ."

THE ATONER *(to* CHRISTIAN*)*: That's right! That's right!! You know what it's like to be really hungry, don't you? It's that kind of hunger for my Word that I want you to have. . .

THE ACCUSER *(to* CHRISTIAN*)*: Ah, come on, man. You're not falling for that ol' gag, are you? I mean, this is the 90's! Live for the moment!

*(*CHRISTIAN *looks up as if hearing something)*

THE ATONER: Read on. . .please. . .read on!

*(*CHRISTIAN *looks down at Bible)*

THE CHRISTIAN: "Blessed are the merciful, for they shall receive mercy. . ."

THE ATONER: Yes. . .yes!

THE ACCUSER: Okay, let Him walk all over you. . .

THE CHRISTIAN: "Blessed are the pure in heart, for they shall see God. . ."

THE ACCUSER: Aha! Check that one out. . .Mr. *(or Miss)* Claim-To-Be-A-Christian-When-It's-Convenient. Well, you remember the times when you were anything but pure. . .

*(*CHRISTIAN *looks up as before: quickly turns the pages of the Bible)*

THE ACCUSER: That's right! Let's get away from that dusty ol' sermon. Read something a little more "today."

THE ATONER *(in a loud whisper to* CHRISTIAN*)*: Ephesians.

THE CHRISTIAN *(thumbing through pages)*: Ephesians. . .Ephesians.

THE ATONER: Good!

THE ACCUSER *(uneasily)*: Ephesians? Uh. . .That's a little deep for you, isn't it?

THE CHRISTIAN: Second Corinthians. . .Galatians. . .here! Ephesians!

THE ATONER: Yes!!

THE CHRISTIAN *(reading)*: "Be strong in the Lord."

THE ACCUSER: Strong? You? Get real. Your track record on strength is not very good, if you'll remember.

THE ATONER: But, I am Lord of your past. . .I died for your sin.

THE ACCUSER: You can't do it. . .you can't be good enough. . .

THE CHRISTIAN *(reading)*: "and in the strength of His might."

THE ATONER: Emphasis on His. I am your strength for today. . .your only hope for tomorrow. . .

THE ACCUSER: You'll never be happy

THE ATONER: You can have real joy

THE ACCUSER: You're doomed

THE ATONER: You're forgiven

THE CHRISTIAN *(reading)*: "Put on the full armor of God. . ."

THE ACCUSER: Uh oh. . .

(THE ACCUSER *begins to try to sneak out*)

THE ATONER/THE CHRISTIAN: "that you may be able to stand firm against the schemes of the devil. . ."

THE ACCUSER *(turning back toward center)*: All right, already! *(exits)*

(THE CHRISTIAN *and* THE ATONER *look at each other and smile, freeze into place; music begins*)

The Armor of God

D. A. and N. A.

DENNIS and NAN ALLEN
Arr. by Dennis Allen

78

80

CD: 54

Broken Places

B. K., D. B. and T. T.

BONNIE KEEN, DARRELL BROWN and TORI TAFF
Arr. by Dennis Allen

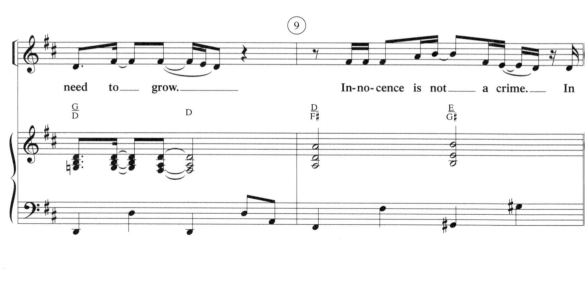

need to_ grow._____ In-no-cence is not___ a crime.___ In

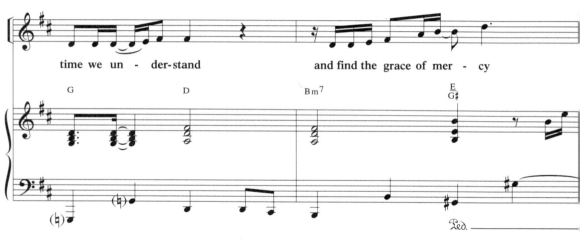

time we un - der-stand and find the grace of mer - cy

sift-ing through the fin - gers of___ God's___ hand.

The Conversation
by Nan Allen

Character:

ANGELA

Props:

telephone

large pillows or bean bag

(Scene opens with ANGELA sitting on stage on pillows or bean bag with the telephone receiver at her ear. She is obviously involved in a telephone conversation.)

Oh come on, Harriet, don't cry. Really, everything's gonna be all right. *(pause)* Well, of course somebody loves you. Uh, who loves you? Well. . .*(pause)* Uh, Harriet, can you hold on for just a second? I've got another call coming in. Hold on. Don't hang up, okay? And try not to cry. What's that, Harriet? Well, get a Kleenex. *(presses button on phone, shakes her head, presses button again)* Hello. Yes, this is Angela. *(pause; sits up straight; in total awe)* Who?!? This is. . .*(gulps)* God? As in "Almighty God"? Uh huh. I mean, yes, sir. Of course, I do recognize the voice, but you're calling me on the phone? *(pause)* I see. Yes, sir, I have been kind of busy lately. You're right. . .not really busy, I've just been on the phone a lot. *(apologetic smile)* Sorry about that. Yes sir, "call waiting" is a nice feature. Modern technology is exciting and I see you're using it to your advantage. *(pause)* Yes, of course, it was all your idea anyway. *(nervous laugh then pauses)* Oh well, God, I'm on another line right now. You see, I have this friend named Harriet and she's . . .yes sir, of course you know all about it. See, Harriet is upset. . .and she's asked me for help. And well. . .*(pause)* Oh, that's what you wanted to talk to me about. Yes, sir. You wanted to remind me that. . .that you love me. Yes, sir. I love You, too. . .and that I need to tell Harriet that You love her, too. *(pause)* But, God, what if she doesn't believe it? She's really upset. *(pause)* Yes, sir. Then I need to show her how you've changed my life. *(pause)* Yes, sir. I know the old saying, "A picture's worth a thousand words." Yes, I suppose that does apply to the Christian life. *(pauses hesitantly)* Uh, Lord, can you stay on the line? I'm gonna need your help. *(pauses and smiles)* Thanks. . .*(presses button on phone twice)* Hello, Harriet, are you still there? Hey, Harriet. . .I've got something I've been meaning to tell you.

(Music begins)

Let Me Show What Love Can Do

D. A. and N. A.

DENNIS and NAN ALLEN
Arr. by Dennis Allen

Let me show what love can do.

1. Lord, in this day and time,
2. In ev - 'ry cir - cum-stance,

CD: 62

1. Lord, in this day and time, Real love is hard to
2. In ev - 'ry cir - cum - stance, Lord, give me ev - 'ry
Real love is hard to find.
Lord, give me ev - 'ry chance.

Let me show___ what___ love can do. Let me show___ it; let me prove_____

what it means___ to be loved by You. Let me show___ what love can,

let me show___ what___ love can do. Let me show____ it; let me prove_____

94

Solid as the Rock

L. B. and G. T.

LARRY BRYANT and GEOFF THURMAN
Arr. by Dennis Allen

98

world a-round__ us drifts and chang - es,_____ Our faith is

sol - id as_ the Rock_ of_ A - ges._____ We re -

joice in__ time when our tri - als__ come. As they test our__ faith, we grow

100

102

*Words by Edward Mote
Tune by William Bradbury

The Ride of Your Life by Nan Allen

Characters:
  WOMAN EXECUTIVE
  CAB DRIVER

Props:
  two chairs, one behind the other, sides to audience
  newspaper
  briefcase with business papers, computer print-outs

(Scene opens with CAB DRIVER *sitting in "driver's seat" reading newspaper. Enter* WOMAN, *hailing cab)*

WOMAN: Taxi! Taxi! *(she opens "cab door" and sits down in back seat)* Finally! Do you know how long I've been. . .

DRIVER *(ignoring her comments; he puts down newspaper)*: Where to, ma'am?

WOMAN: Anywhere!

DRIVER: Anywhere, ma'am?

WOMAN *(agitated)*: Yes, anywhere. . .anywhere I can find some serenity, that is.

DRIVER: Serenity, ma'am?

WOMAN *(aggravated)*: You know, peace and quiet!

*(*DRIVER *nods his head and "drives" in silence)*

WOMAN *(opens briefcase and begins looking at computer print-outs)*: Let's see. . .okay, profit margins! Cash flow!

DRIVER *("stopping the car")*: That'll be $2.40, ma'am.

WOMAN: Here already? *(looks out "cab window" toward audience)* What is this, some kind of sick joke? This is a cemetery!!

DRIVER: Yes, ma'am. You wanted peace and quiet.

WOMAN: Don't be ridiculous. I've totally stressed out right now! You know what kind of peace I'm looking for. . .and surely you know a place where I can find it!!

DRIVER: Yes, ma'am. *("driving" on)* As a matter of fact, I do.

WOMAN *(looking again at computer print-outs)*: Idiot!!

DRIVER *(startled)*: Ma'am? *("stops" car)*

WOMAN *(ignoring driver, speaks aloud to herself)*: Imbecile! Benton takes over that department for two months and WHAM *(pounds the briefcase closed)* they're already behind. I'm gonna kill him. No, I'll fire him first, then I'll kill him. *(to driver)* What have you stopped for?

DRIVER: Making sure you want to go on.

WOMAN: Of course, I do. *(softening)* I need some relief. . .some hope. *(suddenly agitated)* That means no more cemeteries!

DRIVER: Yes, ma'am.

(Silently "drives", then "stops" the car)

DRIVER: We're here, ma'am.

WOMAN: Finally! *(looks out "window" toward audience)* Wait a minute. Where are we? This is a hill with a. . .a. . .cross on top of it. This is some kind of execution. There's a man on that cross. *(with horror)* He's dying!

DRIVER: Yes, ma'am. It's Jesus. You know, God's Son.

WOMAN: Why, this is barbaric!!

DRIVER: Barbaric, ma'am?

WOMAN: Cruel! It's just. . .just. . .

DRIVER: Grace, ma'am?

WOMAN: I don't understand. Why did you bring me here?

DRIVER: Well, ma'am, you said you wanted peace. You wanted relief. You wanted hope. This is the place.

WOMAN: But. . .isn't there any other way? I mean, can't I just take a pill or see a shrink. . .or just go to church sometimes?

DRIVER: No, ma'am. Lots of people have tried those things. This is the place you've been looking for.

WOMAN *(thoughtful silence)*: Can I just stay here in the car?

DRIVER: No, ma'am. You have to take the first step.

WOMAN *(gets out of car on audience side, looks hesitantly, but with her eyes fixed on the "cross"; suddenly remembering, turns toward driver)*: Oh, what do I owe you?

DRIVER: Nothing, ma'am. (looking toward "cross") This one's already been paid for. . .

(all freeze; music begins)

In Christ Alone

S. H. and D. K.

SHAWN CRAIG and DON KOCH
Arr. by Dennis Allen

108

(30) His ten-der mer-cy could reach be-yond my weak-ness to my need.____

(30) Cadd9   Dm11   Am7   Gsus   G

(33) Now,   I__ seek no great-er hon - or   than just to know__ Him

(33) F   F/A   G7/B   F/C   C   F/A   C/G

(36) more,   and to count my gains but loss - es   to the

Fadd9   (36) Fadd9/G   C/E